SILVER INVESTING IN THE SILVER STATE

*Nevada Mining Companies
Ready to Shine.*

By

Mickey Dee

publication is strictly prohibited, and any storage of this document is not allowed unless with written permission from the publisher. All rights reserved.

The information provided herein is stated to be truthful and consistent, in that any liability, in terms of inattention or otherwise, by any usage or abuse of any policies, processes, or directions contained within is the sole and utter responsibility of the recipient reader. Under no circumstances will any legal responsibility or blame be held against the publisher for any reparation, damages, or monetary loss due to the information herein, either directly or indirectly.

Respective authors own all copyrights not held by the publisher.

The information herein is offered for informational purposes solely and is

TABLE OF CONTENTS

INTRODUCTION

Take a second to acknowledge this: Gold and silver bars were still being used as currency even before the first coins were ever produced. Silver has been understood as something that has value across different cultures and thousands of years.

Silver is still a vital commodity today for industrial as well as investment purposes. We will look at those uses in the book. A number of investors don't really understand what makes silver such a valuable commodity.

Sometimes referred to as "the gold of a poor man," silver has been reduced to playing second fiddle behind its shiny yellow equivalent, perhaps a little unfairly. But, as we are about to find out, the precious metal has plenty to give to the planet besides its widespread usage of jewelry and investments.

Silver is one of the important precious metals used by ancient cultures throughout history as the second gold of significance and value. Like Gold, it has always been used as a monetary standard, and there have been found worldwide ancient silver ornaments and silverware that date back centuries.

We've talked about gold and precious metals before, but silver deserves a special mention. Silver is one of Earth's most significant elements and one of the most valuable metals in modern society. The big electrical and thermal conductive properties of Silver are ideal for electrical applications, rendering it extremely taxing in our strongly technology-based environment. You may know it or not, silver plays an immense role in our everyday lives, and we will look at where and how.

Gold is called a precious metal, so in terms of the application of interest, silver along with gold, platinum, and palladium, they form the top 4. Gold has a smooth, shiny, lustrous look, which is derived from the surface of the Earth. Silver shows the maximum electrical conductivity, thermal conductivity, and reflectivity of any metal and as you will read below, this is useful in many applications!

Silver is very malevolent and ductile and easy to work with. It is, however, highly immune to strain, and bends easily. For this purpose, silver is alloyed to improve its hardness and longevity with other metals.

Traditionally, silver jewelry, ornaments, and silverware are made from Sterling Metal. Sterling Silver is an alloy made up of 92.5 percent silver and the remaining 7.5 percent other, usually copper, metals. Items produced from Sterling Silver are typically etched with letters 925, showing a silver value of 92.5 percent.

Sterling Gold is stronger than plain Gold, which is more robust. Often, the Sterling Silver jewelry is plated with an incredibly thin coating of pure silver to add additional shine. Vermeil, found in jewelry, is Sterling Silver covered with a thin film of gold or even platinum. It is an inexhaustible alternative to the valuable metals which it is coated with.

Silver is infamous for its tarnishing habits. New Silver has a bright-metallic-white color, but constant exposure to air almost always becomes yellowish to blackish. This is caused by a silver chemical reaction to the surface sulfur compounds. Glaze the silver with an anti-Tarnish coat is the only way to prevent this impact. Even silver should be kept away from sulfur-rich chickens. Tarnished silver can be easily returned to its original color, using readily available Tarnish-removing chemicals.

The Use of Silver

Silver is made into rings, bracelets, earrings, necklaces, and other figures of jewelry. The majority of metal, though, heads towards being used as ornamental utensils. Goblets, candelabras, cutlery, trays, dishes, and, of course, silverware, are only a few reminders of what makes Silver. Since the earliest times, Silver has been used in coinage too.

Silver has been used in jewelry, food, and currency for centuries, but it can do so much more!

Silver is found in more than 10,000 products – from microchips to microwaves.

Electronics – Silver is an essential part of electrical switches that control your electronics and is commonly used in high-end electronic devices, printed circuits, and audio/video components.

Medicine-Silver is an antimicrobial material, which is commonly used in the medical industry for surgical instruments coating, with wrapping. And of course millions of people have their teeth filled with silver.

Solar Panels – The growing solar energy industry drives demand for silver that is used in the photovoltaic cells of the light-capturing panels, projected to increase that demand.

Mirrors – Mirror-mirror on the wall, gold may be the best metal of all, but behind it all is silver. It's not just hanging on your wall, it's also being used in state-of-the-art telescopes in space far out!

And even more!

HOW IS SILVER USED IN DAILY LIFE?

Silver uses go as far as the ancient times when kingdoms were relying on silver as a form of money. Compared with other precious metals, silver is easy to find, which makes it very popular. Compared to other precious metals such as gold, it often costs less. Why, instead, is it found in daily life? Silver serves a variety of purposes in electronic companies, jewelry companies, and even in the medical sector.

The use of silver in jewelry goes back to the early days. Due to the unique properties that the precious metal exhibits, it is famous in the industry. Silver may be conveniently shaped into various shapes. Thus they usually combine it to form alloys with other metals like copper. The resulting compound may be polished by silversmiths to create rings, necklaces, watch straps, earrings, and much more.

Industrial implementation uses more than 10.000 of silver. Silver has two unique features; high thermal and electrical conductivity, which will make a significant contribution to the industrial and electrical sectors. Now let's see how silver can use everyday life differently.

✓ Antibiotic silver: its efficiency increases dramatically when silver salts are added to antibiotics. Silver can reduce resistance to the bacteria by making it easy for the antibiotic to kill them.

✓ Door handles: These are now coated in silver to prevent the spread of bacteria. As people touch the door with their palm, their saliva activates the silver ions, and the bacteria can't resist because of those ions.

✓ Solar panels: The solar panels are mostly 20 g platinum. Over the past ten years, this market has practically not developed, and today silver demand in the solar industry is increasing significantly as an energy substitute.

✓ Switch of temperature: Silver iodide is also used under extreme situations. This sort of climate engineering releases airborne compounds (silver iodide or dry ice) to raise cloud condensation in the air normally to carry a kind of rain or snow.

- ✓ Photography: Silver is still used in color film photography, although it is not so common these days. Due to their light-sensitive properties, silver halides are used in a gelatin cycle with glass and paper to handle video.

- ✓ Use in mirrors: reflective mirror surfaces are made using a 'silvering' process. While aluminum is a cheap metal to use, only ~90 percent of the light is reflected. Iron, with one of the maximum reflectivity degrees, displays up to 95 percent – 99 percent of light when added to a mirror as an optical cap.

- ✓ Cleansing of the swimming pool: moving over chlorine, no more burning eyes, dry skin, or strong chemical smell. More and more people are now using copper / silver electric ionizing units as an alternative to chlorine for swimming pools. Mineral Pure is one such software maker.

✓ Refrigerators: Samsung has developed a range of refrigerators utilizing silver nana to help secure and conserve food as a shield from harmful bacteria and organism production.

✓ Air conditioning: A / C systems with cool, new air also comes with silver ion filters. Through producing silver ions that kill bacteria, fungi, and other contaminants, these filters tend to reduce air pollutants.

✓ Footwear: silver coated insoles or leather has the rare potential to kill bacteria and odor ideal for sneakers and athletic wear. Shoes of both kinds may benefit from driving, climbing, or exercise.

✓ Money: Gold has been used as currency in the past by many civilizations. The Ottoman Empire (as mite), The Roman Empire, used this stuff. E.I.

WHY IS NEVADA THE SILVER STATE?

Whether or not you attended last month's American Exploration and Mining Meeting in Reno, Nevada, silver investors may still benefit a little more from learning about the mining and mineral background in the great state of Nevada.

First, it is recognized as the Sagebrush State and Battle-Born State, but by a third title, you actually recognize Nevada: the Silver State.

The "Nevada's Nickname" is the State of Silver from Nevada's silver rush of the mid-1800s. Silver was practically picked off the ground in Nevada, with thick gray silver crusts formed on the desert surface for millions of years, transformed by dust and wind into the perfect luster of cow-horns. A big silver bed may be tens of meters deep, and longer than one kilometer.

A decade ago, the bicentennial commemorative quarter of the US Mint for Nevada included wild mustangs, trees, rising sun, sagebrush, and the slogan of the town: The Silver Kingdom.

The Nevada Mining Association credits silver deposits into the mid-nineteenth century as the key to statehood and a driving force in the state economy. And today, mining is vitally essential to their economy. The mining industry in Nevada directly employed over 11,000 workers in the metal ore mining sector, as listed in its most recent report for 2015. Nevada's gold production accounted for 77.6 percent of the U.S. total, according to that report, and helped make the U.S. the world's fourth-leading gold producer in 2015. Alone, Nevada accounted for 5.4 percent of world gold production.

There are currently 24 metals mine sites and 24 mineral industrial sites. A map of mine locations in Nevada can be accessed here. The map was compiled by the Mines and Geology Bureau of Nevada (www.nbmg.unr.edu), and the Minerals Division of Nevada (www.minerals.state.nv.us).

As in any mining operation, miners are seeking solutions for rapid geochemical analysis that will allow them to increase rates of discovery success, quickly identify drill targets, make on-site decisions on whether to stop or keep on going drilling and decide where to focus on the grid. Miners also need to get the capital markets an accurate report as quickly as possible. Portable fluorescence X-ray (XRF) analyzers can make a critical difference in exploration and production of mines. These analyzers provide fast, on-site qualitative screening directly in-situ or quantitative analysis of laboratory content on prepared samples, bypassing the expensive and time-consuming method of sending samples to off-site laboratories and waiting days, or even months, for crucial results. You get real-time geochemical data with rapid sample analysis to drive drilling decisions, enable high-productivity operations, and gain a competitive edge.

10 Things to Know About Nevada

The City of Silver is the home of gold also.

1. 1. The nickname of Nevada 'THE SILVER STATE' was discovered in silver in the town in 1859 and later the migration boom took over the area. Other state nicknames include "Sagebrush Territory" and "Fight Born County.".

2. The state of Silver is also renowned for its gold. Nevada is the world's fourth-largest gold producer and produces around 75 percent of all gold produced in the U.S. Copper and black opals are also common natural resources in Nevada.

3. 3. In 1864 it made known as the first state of which the 15th amendment was passed of 1869 and allowed African American people to vote, years later, it was the 36th state. It allowed African-Americans to vote. The amendment was made a part of the U.S. In 1870, Iowa was the 28th territory to ratify the Constitution.

4. The Spanish gave its name to Nevada in the early 1800s. This came from the Spanish "Sierra Nevada," meaning "mountain range filled in snow."

5. The popular Las Vegas Strip in Nevada is not based in the city in Las Vegas. The Strip is located directly south of Las Vegas and extends almost 4.2 miles across the unincorporated cities of Winchester and Paradise.

6. When it was the first state to have a predominantly female legislature in 2018, Nevada made history. For the 63 legislature positions occupied by the state, 50.8 percent are filled by women.

7. In 1872 a tailor named Jacob Davis designed the blue jeans, initially dubbed "waist overalls," in Reno. Davis took the design to his manufacturer, Levi Strauss & Co., for his creation, which added rivets for extra sturdiness, and the firm charged to register his patent claim, which was issued in 1873.

8. Bordered by Oregon, Idaho, California, Utah, and Arizona, Nevada is the seventh-largest state by population. The federal government controls around 85 percent of the property,

including the isolated location of Area 51, situated northwest of Las Vegas, founded by the Central Intelligence Agency in 1955.

9. A total of 96 men died when the Hoover Dam was built, which was the world's tallest dam at its completion in 1935.

10. The businesses based in Nevada include Wynn Resorts, Allegiant Air, MGM Resorts International, Zappos, and Bally Technologies. While mining is the largest export industry of the state, aerospace and defense are the other main industries in the state-agriculture, information technology, oil, safety, tourism, and gaming. The city has also welcomed major sports teams like the Las Vegas Knights in the National Hockey League (NHL), The

Las Vegas Raiders in the National Football League (NFL) and the Las Vegas Aces of the Women's National Basketball Association (WNBA).

WHY IS MINING IMPORTANT TO NEVADA?

Since 1990, the mining industry has added over $100 million to Nevada and local economies per year. This is especially important for rural economies; in rural Nevada, mining is the largest industry. Due to mining, revenues from Washoe and Clark counties are not required to help the state's agricultural regions, so mining generates several well-paying employment for rural populations. Total contributions to the state and municipal governments from mining firms in Nevada in 2014, minus any taxes charged from manufacturers or workers, is $245.8 million.

Nevada mining has been supplying minerals for more than 150 years and is vital to a creative and developed community. Today the Silver State mines over 20 minerals. These minerals are present in thousands of daily things that we use. Electronic equipment, transportation methods, and the buildings in which we live and work are just a few examples of how mining advantages our lives. As emerging innovations keep changing the globe, the original STEM (science, technology, engineering and math) industry from Nevada has provided the minerals required to help shape the future of our country.

The great mineral riches of Nevada founded this remarkable geographic area as a state almost 150 years ago and continue to be an important field of the economy of the State. Mining is Nevada's main manufacturing sector, due to world-class reserves of gold, silver and other minerals.

Perhaps best known for its development of gold, silver, and copper, Nevada is a significant source of a number of minerals, such as lithium, iron, and molybdenum, essential for the manufacturing of consumer and industrial products that are so relevant to our contemporary lifestyles. Many industrial materials used in buildings are present in abundance in Nevada, such as gypsum, calcareous, clay, and gravel. Also, geothermal heat is exploited for power production, with one of the biggest geothermal fields in the country.

Nevada's mining industry in the 19th century was a key driver of industrial development and continues to fuel technical and scientific progress. The

Mackay College of Earth Sciences and Mining at the University of Nevada, located in Reno, is one of the world's leading mining colleges. They produce six-figure mining engineers every year.

Around 12,000 employees in Nevada's mining industry are directly working mainly in rural Nevada and are paying some of the highest annual wages, totaling 83,000 dollars in the state. Mining often includes a robust program of assistance. Around four other industries provide supplies and facilities provided by the mining sector for most of the mining workers.

Chances are all of the things you use every day include a piece of Nevada. Nevada's minerals, used in construction materials, machines, batteries, and a number of other items too numerous to name, are important to everyday life around the world. And the London Olympics awards shone even bigger, due to gold from Nevada.

SILVER COMPANIES IN THE SILVER STATE

LOCATION   SALES REVENUE ($M)
Barrick Goldstrike Mines Inc.   Elko, Nevada, United
States of America

$838.19M

Coeur-Rochester, Inc.   Coeur D' Alene, Idaho, United
States of America

129.53M

Barrick Turquoise Ridge Inc. Golconda, Nevada,
United States of America

$82.19M

Meridian Gold Inc.   Reno, Nevada, United States
of America

$64.06M

Mervine Mining Company   Henderson, Nevada,
United States of America

$60.00M

Round Mountain Gold Corp   Round Mountain,
Nevada, United States of America

$57.64M

Veris Gold USA Inc.   Elko, Nevada, United States of
America

$57.64M

Florida Canyon Mining, Imlay, Nevada, United States
of America

$51.35M

Jerritt Canyon Gold LLC   Elko, Nevada, United States of America

$37.20M

Turquoise Ridge Mining Company Golconda, Nevada, United States of America

$35.03M

Cortez Gold Corporation   Beowawe, Nevada, United States of America

$33.81M

Hycroft Resources & Development, Inc .Winnemucca, Nevada, United States of America

$33.07M

Newmont USA Limited Elko, Nevada, United States of America

$31.81M

Rawhide Mining LLC Fallon, Nevada, United States of America

$21.12M

Rare Gold Rocks LLC   Stateline, Nevada, United States of America

$11.50M

KG Mining (Bald Mountain) Inc.   Ely, Nevada, United States of America

$10.78M

Meridian Gold Company   Reno, Nevada, United States of America

$10.55M

Pershing Gold Corporation Lakewood, Colorado, United States of America

$3.97M

Barrick Golden Sunlight Elko, Nevada, United States of America

$2.94M

A.U. Mines, Inc. Reno, Nevada, United States of America

$2.80M

Elko Mining Group, LLC   Reno, Nevada, United States of America

$1.86M

Scorpio Gold (us) Corporation Elko, Nevada, United States of America

$1.73M

Gryphon Gold Corporation Reno, Nevada, United States of America

$1.56M

Kapacke Mining, LLC   Las Vegas, Nevada, United States of America

$1.47M

Klondex Gold & Silver Mining Company Winnemucca, Nevada, United States of America

$1.09M

Cortez Barrick Inc Beowawe, Nevada, United States of America

$0.98M

Desert Hawk Gold Corp.   Reno, Nevada, United States of America

$0.89M

Patriot Gold Corp. Las Vegas, Nevada, United States of America

$0.88M

Just Equipment Inc	Sparks, Nevada, United States of America
	$0.53M
Wellard Industrial L.L.C.	Spring Creek, Nevada, United States of America
	$0.35M
Blessed Diamonds Inc	Las Vegas, Nevada, United States of America
	$0.30M
Plum Mining Co LLC	Virginia City, Nevada, United States of America
	$0.30M
Kinross Gold USA Inc	Reno, Nevada, United States of America
	$0.30M
Marshall Earth Resources, Inc.	Virginia City, Nevada, United States of America
	$0.28M
Nevada Pacific Gold (us) Inc	Elko, Nevada, United States of America
	$0.25M
Discovery Dynamics Incorporated	Sparks, Nevada, United States of America
	$0.25M
Paramount Gold and Silver Corp.	Winnemucca, Nevada, United States of America
	$0.23M
Gold Acquisition Corp	Lakewood, Colorado, United States of America
	$0.22M

Twin Creeks Mine   Winnemucca, Nevada,
United States of America

$0.21M

Lode-Star Mining Inc.   Reno, Nevada, United States
of America

$0.20M

Rawhide Mining, LLC   Fallon, Nevada, United States
of America

$0.19M

GRC Nevada Inc   Fernley, Nevada, United
States of America

$0.18M

Comstock Mining Inc.   Virginia City, Nevada, United
States of America

$0.18M

Ensurge, Inc.   Reno, Nevada, United States of
America

$0.17M

Rimrock Gold Corp.   Las Vegas, Nevada, United
States of America

$0.15M

Nevada Rand LLC   Fallon, Nevada, United States
of America

$0.14M

Dimension Resources (USA) Inc.   Reno, Nevada,
United States of America

$0.14M

Grizzly Gold Corp.   Reno, Nevada, United States
of America

$0.13M

Cibolan Gold Corporation Reno, Nevada, United
States of America

$0.13M

Black Hawk Exploration   Las Vegas, Nevada,
United States of America

$0.11M

Tap Resources, Inc.   Carson City, Nevada, United
States of America

$0.10M

Silver Rock Recovery   Las Vegas, Nevada, United
States of America

$0.10M

Trulan Resources Inc.   Henderson, Nevada, United
States of America

$0.09M

Preston Corp.   Carson City, Nevada, United
States of America

$0.09M

Tundra Gold Corp.   Reno, Nevada, United States
of America

$0.09M

Nevada Gold Mines LLC   Elko, Nevada, United
States of America

$0.09M

Canyon Gold Corp.   Las Vegas, Nevada, United
States of America

$0.09M

Advantego Corporation   Elko, Nevada, United States of America

$0.08M

Silver Reserve Corp.   Reno, Nevada, United States of America

$0.07M

Ranger Gold Corp.   Reno, Nevada, United States of America

$0.07M

National Gold Mining Corp Reno, Nevada, United States of America

$0.07M

Gracepoint Mining Corp. Henderson, Nevada, United States of America

$0.04M

Paramount Gold Nevada Corp. Winnemucca, Nevada, United States of America

$0.03M

Nevada Canyon Gold Corp.   Reno, Nevada, United States of America

$0.01M

Uscorp Carson City, Nevada, United States of America

$0.00M

U.S. Gold Corp. Elko, Nevada, United States of America $0.00M

Dakota Territory Resource Corp.   Reno, Nevada, United States of America

$0.00M

Mexus Gold US Carson City, Nevada, United States of America

$0.00M

Silver Standard U.S. Services Inc. Valmy, Nevada, United States of America

$0.00M

Placer Dome North America Elko, Nevada, United States of America

$0.00M

Newmont Goldcorp Corporation Golconda, Nevada, United States of America

$0.00M

Barrick Turquoise Ridge Inc.   Elko, Nevada, United States of America

$0.00M

Barrick Gold of North America, Inc. Henderson, Nevada, United States of America

$0.00M

Barrick Goldstrike Mines Inc. Carlin, Nevada, United States of America

$0.00M

Barrick Turquoise Ridge Inc. Golconda, Nevada, United States of America

$0.00M

Barrick Goldstrike Mines Inc. Elko, Nevada, United States of America

$0.00M

Barrick Turquoise Ridge Inc. Elko, Nevada, United States of America

$0.00M

Newmont Goldcorp Corporation Battle Mountain, Nevada, United States of America

$0.00M

Newmont Corporation Elko, Nevada, United States of America

$0.00M

Newmont Mining Corporation Elko, Nevada, United States of America

$0.00M

Newmont Goldcorp Corporation Winnemucca, Nevada, United States of America

$0.00M

Newmont Goldcorp Corporation Battle Mountain, Nevada, United States of America

$0.00M

Newmont Goldcorp Corporation Valmy, Nevada, United States of America

$0.00M

N.A. Degerstrom, Inc.   Elko, Nevada, United States of America

$0.00M

Coeur-Rochester, Inc.   Lovelock, Nevada, United States of America

$0.00M

BONUS: Baby Knockouts & More for Your Watch list

The following list includes Baby Knockouts. For you that have never listened to The Scoop with Mickey Dee on YouTube, Baby Knockouts are companies that have something special about them and our research indicates that they have the ability to execute and dominate a particular area. They can have a special technology or great management team. They may have a massive resource deposit in a certain area of the world or simply have great assets in a depressed industry. They are usually under .25 USD. I coined the term Baby Knockout while trading the Dotcoms in the early 90's. The first Baby Knockout was America Online (AOL) which went from .25 to over $1000 split adjusted. We currently have many Baby Knockouts on the move including Ely Gold Royalty from .08 to over $1.50, Applied DNA Sciences from .25 to over $13 and NexTech AR Solutions from .25 to $4.60. We are anticipating a very robust mining Baby Knockout season and the silver Baby Knockouts may be the best performers of them all! Here they are:

Discovery Metals (DSVMF/DSV.V) $217M Market Cap

Falco Resources (FPRGF/FPC.V) $77M Market Cap

Golden Minerals Company (AUMN) $45.8M Market Cap

Aurcana Corp (AUNFF) (AUN.V) $81.3M Market Cap

Silver One Resources (SLVRF) (SVE.V) $58.4M Market Cap

Southern Silver Exploration Corp (SSVFF) (SSV.V) $19.3M Market Cap

Avino Silver & Gold (ASM) (ASM.TO) $47.4M Market Cap

Dolly Varden Silver Corp (DOLLF) $27.6 Market Cap

Callinex Mines (CLLXF) (CNX.V) (CAXA.F) $9.0 Market Cap

Defiance Silver Corp (DNCVF) (DEF.V) (D4E.MU) (D4E.F) $21.1M Market Cap

Aftermath Silver (AAGFF) (AAG.V) $19.9M Market Cap

Endeavour Silver Corp (EXK) (EDR.TO) (EJD.F) (EJD.MU) $296.4M Market Cap

Impact Silver (ISVLF) (IPT.V) (IKL.F) (IKL.MU) (IKL.DU) $52M Market Cap

WORTHY BABY KNOCKOUTS HONORABLE

MENTION

Excellon Resources (EXXLF / EXN.TO) – One of Mexico's highest grade silver producers, $83M Market Cap

Treasury Metals (TSRMF / TML.TO / TRC.BE / TRC.F) a well funded exploration company in Canada. Potentially explosive small cap! $62M Market Cap

Mako Mining – (MAKOF / MKO.V) Insider buying recently. It's one of the leading miners in Nicaragua. $187M Market Cap

Midas Gold (MDRPF / MAX.TO) great gold project in United States, $129M Market Cap

Revival Gold (RVLGF / RVG.V) Idaho and Utah gold projects. $41M Market Cap

GR Silver Mining (GRSLF / GRSL.V / GPE.F) former Strata Minerals. Projects located in United States, $46M Market Cap.

Do not go yet; One Last Thing to Do

If you enjoyed this book or found it useful, I'd be very grateful if you'd post a short review on Amazon. Your support really does make a difference, and I read all the reviews personally so I can get your feedback and make this book even better.

Thanks again for your support!

About the Author:

Mickey "Dee" Frazier is a stock and real estate investor, independent researcher, freelance writer and You Tuber. His company, Frazier Publishing & Services relocated from Hollywood, California to North Las Vegas, NV in 2009. Frazier Publishing & Services has published over 150 paperback, audio and eBooks including numerous best sellers. You can sign up free and see his weekly updates on YouTube: https://www.youtube.com/user/mickeyf5 12